Aidan Semmens, former co-editor of *Perfect Bound* magazine and winner of the 1978 Chancellor's Medal for an English Poem at Cambridge, read of himself in *Jacket* in 2002 that he had "long given up writing poetry". His work has since been in *Shearsman, Stride, Shadowtrain, Jack, Jacket, Great Works, Blackbox Manifold, Free Verse, Otoliths* and *Likestarlings*. He lives in Suffolk, where some of his photographs have been exhibited at the Snape Maltings gallery.

A Stone Dog

Aidan Semmens

Shearsman Books

First published in the United Kingdom in 2011 by
Shearsman Books Ltd
58 Velwell Road
Exeter EX4 4LD

www.shearsman.com

ISBN 978-1-84861-165-8
First Edition

Cover photograph by the author.

Acknowledgements

Poems in this collection have appeared in the following magazines:
Blackbox Manifold (Damaged Mirror, Relics); *Free Verse* (Four
Distressed Sonnets); *Great Works* (In Tombland, Depicting The Artist
As, From Afar, Where Is He That Counted The Towers, And Brake
Them Beneath The Mount, Torch Song); *Jack* (On the Curlew River,
Wave); *Jacket* (Lamentation, Upon the Death of John Barleycorn);
Shadowtrain (In The Process, Phenomenology, The Uncertainty
Principle); *Shearsman* (In Passing, What Then Must We Do,
The Penitents, How Doth the City Sit Solitary I); and
Stride (As Far As I Can See, The Pleasure Beach).

'The Good News' is a reworking of material that appeared in 1985
in the Pig Press Staple Diet pamphlet *Confidential Report*.

Contents

In memory of Ric Caddel

A Stone Dog

From Afar

byline on the author photo
provides a place to start:
he pretty, monochrome
she a mystery merely a name
maybe Malay

slight hint of a distant
land of water, stilted homes

then there is a handwritten
inscription on the flyleaf
but that tells us nothing

the depths to which I
    depths or heights
it was ever

these are extraordinary times we
—always they are, times, extraordinary
extratemporal

the sun setting quicker
tideline shifting
contours mobile on the map

call of curlew nocturnal

mildew & must
a suspicion
moisture of empire
has entered the pages

The Pleasure Beach

gummed wrapping, fresh
—twenty-four exciting
new flavours,
cultural references
to collect

timeless representations
of human truths,
opera, shadow or mirror images,
a dialogue of Dionysian
abandon
            distant rewards of Time,
immediate delights of Pleasure
the only constant ambiguity

Pleasure salutes to Pain

when one's childish fingers stumbled
through the works of Zemlinsky
that bridge atonal
& serial works
influences & cultural milestones
two forms
            of cryptic
message communication: enigmatic
utterings of Delphi,
spy number transmissions
on the shortwave radio

an abandoned
            military building
where blocks of colour meet
I was reminded of painting

Master William turns the handle
& notes come. It is a Player
Piano—that is, a piano
without a player

at noon, on every Sunday
something happens
a bizarre piece of art
Breaking the Code—something
weird
          & wonderful: false
colour satellite image of Suffolk: colours—
dark, very dark red/black,
coniferous trees; black/blue
water; blue urban areas,
bare earth. In various
order ranged as Time
sets all things right

at noon, on every Sunday
& then
let's be fashionable
& say art died
flawed & driven genius haunts me,
symbolist poetry & a rich
palette of sounds,
short grim apocalyptic
portent of war

Ophelia's journey into madness,
symbolic voyage through love,
rarely heard
               mythology & sounds
in an essay of exoticism,
elegant phrasing, glistening

fingerwork
only faith that is necessary,
lushly welcoming Death

an age of tension & anxiety
—not Bolshevik illiterates but men
with a musically educated ear
—Balzac, Proust—all that
is sociology,
                    predominantly
quiet sonorities

Having an avid interest in all varieties
of arcane weaving
                    of the Middle East,
chevaux-de-frise, portable barriers
of spikes designed
to check cavalry charges—
Samuel Beckett's favourite
piece of music was Schubert's Death
& the Maiden

taken from a ballet & full
of lurching waltz rhythms,
every utterance a distillation,
prime heather-covered heathland
sea views from the cliffs,
mythological depictions
                    of women
moving through this world
with unearthly ease
waterproof footwear is essential

I suspect never again
will I carry a marimba across a beach,

cut swathes
through the intellectual fabric of Britain
born in the year
of the October Revolution, he talks
about culture & politics,
distorted dance music
& warped waltzes

embodies a degree of spiritual
searching, earthbound & obvious

an eccentric collection of acts
trapped in a war-torn homeland,
recent responses
to war & peace

at noon, on every Sunday
two forms of cryptic
influences & cultural
milestones, painting
where blocks of colour meet

I know where there's some turnips

On the Curlew River

dawn comes slowly through
phosphorescent mist
creeping across the reedbeds

a red-throated diver sits calm
glacial erratic with a dash of colour
where wavelets edge
at the mudbank shore
of an islet built by silt & reed
river's trickle & tidal seep
meet in a swirl, missing a beat

the round stone tower at the river's bend
is a thumbprint of brown, clumsy
upright in the landscape's horizontal

longship & liner
grey smudge
on grey horizon

grey waves crash on flint, grinding
axehead, keep & cloister
to shingle; bodies washed
up & away, liquor mortis
infinitely dilute

Sins of the Fathers

much that was hidden has come to light,
the still beautiful colours,
the sky behind the Christ, fine
hatching, rusting heads of nails

passion leaves traces
eccentric, wry,
a guy
        who cares

burning issues
from a pipeline, caustic
military intelligence
spooking the spooks

anxious ghosts guided by a book,
spotlight stolen by the struggle

songbirds, flowers, fish & jade,
world-class shopping, years
of colonial rule: talks
still have a chance

allow plenty of time,
shake hands with everyone
English is widely spoken
(speaking Spanish
will cause offence);

take pause for Passover,
read scripture wisely,
proscription of the Pentateuch,
Qu'ranic interpretations,

the Selected Poems of God
the worse it gets
in fractured time
the tighter
           some cling
to their inadequacies,
celibacies
           of the intellect
still doing God's work

war dog sniffing out trouble:
two men on a motorcycle,
a drive-by killing

the papers reveal
scandalous material: 36%
are said to favour an
assassination: 70%
the figure by which
Russia's deathrate
exceeds birthrate—
no longer evil, the empire
is dying

water, gas, telephone, electricity:
their delivery conquered darkness
an icon of empire, internet
pornography, two gunmen
outside a church

           the king
is coming home, the war
is winding down, knives
made of old mortar shells,
great deals

on a Kalashnikov
the fight against violence,
                text dissolved
into a stream of dots—
the revolutionary invention
of a man named Hell

in a small complex of squat brick buildings
a nest of spies
trades information,
                  reviewing the breach,
sanctity of the confessional:
a Tartar paramilitary
training in the hills of Crimea,
holding dear
disbelief, fear,
the image of a martyr

an imperfect peace in the forbidden valley,
messy disputes
                between rival factions—
We're here to kill & destroy—
pitched gun battles at the gates
of the palace
but more than a valley separates them

bodies pile up & the diplomats
scramble, zealots achieving
a placid life—lack of
certainty is exhausting

he doesn't like
to talk politics; lately
she has been picturing her death.

We rode buses. We went
to cafes. He wanders around Bethlehem
looking for work; amnesia
can be dangerous
summer festivals in the mountains, miniskirted
femmes fatales, abandoned
buildings ravaged by gunfire

                        pulsate until dawn

the land of opportunity,
the wisdom of the dead,
business as usual

20 years ago that bastard raped me—
hardly a ringing mea culpa

tears of bereaved mothers,
a jigsaw of tiny fragments—
Massacre of the Innocents
with added figures of the Virtues
& Vices: mysterium iniquitatis

a convertible to match her lipstick
in the cut
         & thrust of
attractive pharmaceuticals
bring a dream to life—
dress, shoe, bag & coat:
fashion with Passion
the challenge
            of Holy Week

it is better
to marry
than to burn

The Good News

daylight a city
surrounded by sand
dipping & rising
through the horizontal

cameras missed the action but caught
the blood & the bandages
routine affective questioning
rubble spills on the paving

shreds of cloth in labelled bags
bright points on the paper
focused through lenses
as we strike the keys

refracting the flames
from wharves
at night in the water's
oily surface

routed across a difficult terrain
innocent rain tumbling in
ravines leaves
falling on a shining lake

fireworks celebrate
old revolutions
mugshots of peasants & conspirators
infiltrators a business party

looks down
as sun glints on snow

a river winding
out of breath

freightways & flightpaths
aides & interpreters
patterns of green & grey
high-rise buildings

shipments of steel
crawling on the sea
chimneysmoke & boys
playing football

across the hallway disturbances
to eavesdrop on
blood from old sores
on the sheets on the walls

yellowed clippings
pasted up keep
your thoughts &
imperfections to yourself

we keep a file on territories
exposed to chemical damage
assess compensation
store information

rearrange the facts
keep order
from the sky
snaking rivers

expose the lie
of the land

wisps of cloud
bisect villages

& farms
casting strange lives
into shadow
cameras level

a steady eye
discover primitive
rites & responsibilities
engage self-appointed

experts to uncover
conspiracies
dip a finger
to fill in pale forms

taste the facts
a mania for detail
the human
stories the truth

a travelogue life
of exotic captures a sense
of decorum prevents
too close an invasion

a cut head
in Mexican stone
watercolour print
of a garden in Japan

a familiar fetish
a token

gesture
of brotherhood

peeling plaster dust
baked earth
pale shining faces
too many bright tones

in the landscape
in the frame
fixed smiles
& bayonets

far-reaching maps
shelved plans
& a living
in the country

through the picture window
we watch the children
play hide & seek with
machineguns & typewriters

voices reflect
from the wharves
& we have a thing
to write home about

For I Have Seen That I Knew Not

the suffering likely to be endured
by the civilian population
the babies born blind
the germ of this macabre idea

probably because I had sat up on a hard seat all night
the guns made a terrible noise

a chilly day not good for observing
deserted ruined streets, deserted roadway
cellars transfigured as dugouts
rubble, rubbish & an old plush chair

meat two days a week, bread & jam for tea
nothing from the bedroom but the trees & a stone dog

Depicting the Artist As

deprived of the elements of speech
in a photo, in front of a wall
the interest of formal relationships
what is the status of feelings?

the self is a site for chaos
emotions are dangerous, but a life without emotion
is not a good one, anomalies of the nervous system—
art based on the faculty of deceit
the style of the poser uncovers a language of posture

one catches sight of her in New York during the Great War
the opening of a risqué Paris nightclub or a clandestine
Surrealist film—amateur & police photos intend to sell nothing
assemblage of art from shards

travel as an elliptical form of quest
we see Allied fighters in formation above a landscape
a life rebuilt from attic fragments
the family photo is deliberately blurred

in seeing these things we see the difficulty of seeing anything
blur & imperfection
the attentive silence as well as the pose
the inadequacy of an inattentive life

deprived of the elements of speech
low-toned & oblique, almost beyond interpretation
the hanging body of Gudrun Ensslin
nothing could be further from the truth

As Far As I Can See

I

the observer is a necessary
part of the landscape
feet mired in sludge of belonging
intrinsic faecal matter
mould of mortal detritus
leaves
fallen
to the matted
carpet

the auditor makes the sound of the forest
a communion
with the bark
lichen & fungus
the light
striking
a droplet
poised
shattering
into tactile solidity
of a rainbow small
enough to fit in the closed palm

the bird is a bird
the thrush is a thrush
the mushroom is a mushroom

II

high in the hill country
peewits parting the air
that mournful cry

rabbit trails in heather
& changing weather
across valley slopes; hope

peters out like pattering hail
a taste of bilberries not yet ripe
clinging unwanted to the tongue

III

I have been dreaming
that my teeth are falling out
Freud would attribute this
to anxiety
about incipient impotence
I think it is because
my teeth are falling out

IV

smoke from a steamer
blends into brown fog
men in duffel coats
wrap clumsy fingers
round steaming sandwiches
of fish grilled on the deck
of the boat that caught them

as they wait for the ferry
that will take them to work

here people have different
expectations, gods
a different way of writing
the same brands of soft drink
holes in the pavement
an unwary or unlucky person
could lose their life in

they have caverns measureless
to man & an economy
of the kind that in some places
leads to hardship & lust
for war

they are happy & they are miserable
their carpets are the finest & their tea the sweetest

nothing resembles anything but itself

V

admire the architecture, crossbeam
& corbel, mullions of a window
only internal
trowelscrapes for fragments
of significance
nothing without
the text
has integrity, responds
to nothing beyond

the beam is not a homage, it's a beam
that holds the splaying walls from falling out

words without reference
    pour concrete, pound piles
word made dialectic
    life & geology in primal churn
word made apparatus
    beauty of the fractal whirr

farmyard cockerel
wind in the pines
a machine buzz

VI

the voyeur is a necessary
part of the experience
toothache in the theatre
integral to the performance

the trees which were heavy with fruit
are bent with snow
breaking boughs echoing
in unpeopled wilderness

you take the knife you cut meat with
to perform an operation on yourself

it is not the sentiment of sunset appals the senses
it is the savour of the earth
at the cool end of a hot day
the sky is bruised & purple

your fingers clipped & raw
the blood tastes metallic in your mouth

then be not afraid, for there is no judgement
what is self-evident is often untrue

Wave

A helicopter lands on the Pan-Am roof
like a dragonfly on a tomb

Photoptosis in deep space
is a kyrie of confused creation.

Jugbands & juggernauts
jig & jag, sending out waves
to be read by whom we know not,
whomsoever it may concern:
it's religion for the teleporter age,
a candle in a windless window,
unoxygenated combustion in a limitless belljar.
Alpha beta gamma light radio
a light programme of light relief,
waving hello to those we don't know
we ever met, waving like corn,
waves crashing in a jetfighter's otic wake,
a permanent wave from a beehive drier,
waves of emotion, heatwave concussion,
waving to someone
out
there,
tripping the light fantastic.

A helicopter lands
on a desert airstrip
like a dragonfly,
scattering sand, a little scrub,
& perhaps a few lizards.
The blades leave a wave
on the earth's surface.

Helicopter: flying machine,
Greek, spiral-winged; Pan-Am,
Pan-American, all-American, from
Greek, pan—all, everything, the
rustic god of all things. Roof,
the top of this. Pan-American,
airline of a great imperial power of
the 20th century, common era: a
collection of flying things—like
helicopter, dragonfly: a dragon
which flies, or a fly
which resembles a dragon? Dragon—
mythological beast. Dragonfly—
anisoptera, Latin. Tomb, room
where we bury our dead. The chill
of the tomb, the silence
broken by a helicopter. Quote:
Joni Mitchell, Canadian entertainer,
jazz-tinged in this period, that
of hissing lawns, the Boho Zone,
the jungle line, Rousseau in the park;
jazz the beat of one continent
in the cities of another. Canada,
a northerly zone of pan-America.
Photoptosis, visible light, from Greek:
a work of music by Zimmerman,
German composer of 20th century,
common era. Deep space, somewhere
far away. Deep, the sea;
space, room, limitless vacuum, vacuity,
lebensraum. Kyrie—from kyrie eleison, Greek,
lord have mercy on us,
a liturgical device, burden
of canonical songs. Creation:
this, the heavens or any other.

Jugbands, from jug, jig or jazz.
Juggernaut, a huge vehicle, of unstoppable
size or momentum, from Jaganath, Hindu,
lord of the world, dragged by thousands
in annual pilgrimage.
Jig & jag, euphony, alliteration, para-rhyme,
hints of Irish dance, a motorcar,
a popular singer, the undulating movement zigzag.
To undulate, from Latin, unda, a wave,
to make little waves. Wave,
a greeting or gesture of farewell;
a characteristic motion of water,
the sea perhaps, or the mode of travel
of light, sound, radio communication,
heat, optimism or fashion,
ripples on a tide of emotion.
A candle, a gesture, incandescence
of flame on wax: oxygen—
without this it cannot live. Combustion
impossible in a belljar, a jar
in which a bell cannot be heard,
its wave extinguished. Teleporter,
from Greek, carrying far. A window,
through which we look out.
A jetfighter, powered component
of an uncivil airline, wing
of an imperial power. Otic,
of the ear. Wake, a wave
made in passing. Alpha, beta,
gamma, waves, from Greek. Radio,
telegraphy that radiates like rods or spokes,
from Latin. Telegraphy, Greek, far drawings.

Desert, a land deserted, unfit
for stable settlement. Airstrip,

man's mark in the sand. Sand
perhaps equals time.
Lizards: an older lifeform.
Scrub: the same, but of another order.
Blades cut, carve air for flight.
The earth's surface: implies surfaces
elsewhere. Religion, mythology, jazz,
photoptosis, imply belief
in waves.

A helicopter lands,
like a dragonfly,
on a tomb.

In the Process

fresh-made with mozzarella
chalkboarded by a rain-
smeared paving

I'm only to blame for believing
the wrong words

we stop
contain paragraph all
the small featureless
things we

fear perhaps is too strong a word

the chip in the mirror, crack
in the fabric of this

life pertains to possibilities
of what

things we cannot
perceive

the chalk marks splashed
& partially
de-written

Phenomenology

Fast poetry promotes shallow breathing
          —Peter Riley

I

awkward as the way he
holds his book
his apparition
in the dark beyond

I was startled
by the sound of his

voice trails mark the dim
night, mere scratches
on the appearance of

red lights
individuated, numerable
in rejection
of the horizontal
blend into one near
straight line
pointing directly

anxiety, love
& all those personal affects

I is the self
a body dreamed
impertinent
as a pebble
recessive golem
recusant ape

II

inconsequential
markers
of a seamless
faith seem
less than
some windblown
particles particularly
among these casually
strewn stones
mono
liths
in an upland
escape
definition &
consequence

behind carious
shutters angles
in offkey
curious
against
lurid sky
light gutter
pipes & rust
stain drape
stucco coming
unstuck

petrified anguish, ossified
decay, what
torment had
the mason artisan
in mind

greened
with lichen, roots
of airborne
herb in precarious
hold at point
of bird-passed nutrient, a howl
but no
emetic capacity

III

failures of registration
within the temporal smear
perception turns imperceptibly
to memory
the unreliable archive
between clairvoyance
& reconstruction

a subjective sequence
of events, degraded
narrative
in phenomenal space
all deviations
are corruptions of the text

take pause for breath
between the skeins of content
weft of conscience
thread of argumentative
response
a felt of dust
builds up against
the needle

all the little sparkplug epiphanies
tugged out
held up
from your tongue
this is the life
but you don't mean
whatever you say

a shallow narrative
promotes fast breathing
the illusion of
pleasure
her red hair
falling
across her face

IV

bread & politics
junk food of a tired nation
loosely defined
by thought, culture, the gods

they do not worship
but respect
the shapes of their windows
the way they write

their names
in the dust of panes
take tea in glasses
perched upon stools of rare design
barely comprehensible to us who
pass through other tunnels, lives

bled out in other
highways & on ledges
of high-rise cities called Despair
or mere Convention

stamped in the fabric
of the very thing I need
or duly wish for
the words made in China
in a language that is not Chinese

V

in which things
explain
each other
not themselves

these hands are those
of my elder sister
younger
mirror shows
my brother
much as he was

don't look away

it is
as if
but not

only of the
thing which

don't
look away

a cup of coffee a landscape
swirled in mist
it makes you think

about this
there's nothing
you can do

so this is how
the puzzle is
solved—you must
choose
where you put your line

VI

junks & sampans on
an oversaturated sea
temples with tassles
TV in the back room
speaks another language
a prayer perhaps
coercion of god

they'll take the words
from your mouth
& use them against you

blood seeping through the pages

In Shanghai

stands, roughly, half a house,
battered brickwork severed to reveal
lately abandoned rooms, shabby paperwork,
plumbing & plaster

grouped around, glowering, prowling
loom predators of sun-caught steel
& glass among my grandfather's
photos, sampans crowd

around a sleek destroyer
come lately from the war
to an imperial presence before
the smoking factories & grand

boulevards of that great port
I still have somewhere
the mah-jong set he traded there
illegally, in my dictionary

to Shanghai someone
means to compel them
into service aboard ship
probably by drugging

Only If

the moonlight strikes it
is the house truly there
& then only if
we are there to see
(& happen to be looking) but what
of the people who live
in the house? for them
it is we who
are eternally absent

if they are there at all
& if
we have not imagined
the house merely

The Uncertainty Principle

*The italicised stanzas in this poem are quotations from,
respectively, Velimir Khlebnikov, Daniel C Dennett,
Hegel & Douglas Dunn*

not as this with
the passages we give ourselves to

inasmuch as this:
the fly wiping its many lenses
with its legs
the madonna's tears
intricately carved
inaccessible of view
the circumscribed space
in which a whisper's echo
magnifies
all meaning & significance
the metaphor for the nucleus & the atom

nuded by chainsaw
& indifference the hillside sweeps
to a different climax, wind
to another beat
vortex of interstices
it fair takes
the breath away

I think I'll love this country more
in its coming dereliction

the particles zoom through timespace
little
do they care

what matter
of opinion or fact they
collide
        with
interpenetrable
interferent
quanta of waving

pin them down
& your tail on the donkey
of what's not out
there

in here
inherent
uncertainty

I don't think god

inasmuch as
discrete entities
within the alpha particle
may coalesce
unremarked
or digress
& scintillate

a tempting path towards the nucleus
the path of high voltage

complaisant into the serial mouth
the cowboy nation stutters:
bomb-blasts bankrolled
bombast treasured

the democratic nations did nothing to help

another day I didn't get
to shoot my gun

the scars this year are late to heal
I feel ungerminated soil
cleave to the rock beneath my feet
the skin sweats
I sense its pallor
innocent of the unforgiving sun

adamantine surfaces
withhold their tensile purpose
on which you slip
                there is
no empathy in stone, no cause
for which the crystal structure breaks
no hidden motive, no
propensity for pain

consciousness & conscience derive from chaos
chance effusions of the particle dance

tick-tock
tick
    & tock

the magic in a word
remains even if
it is not understood

caught in sublimity of encoded longing
we fake our encryption of a facile world
see carp swim

in the carpal tunnel
vision of our ineradicable
deficiencies
differences
of opinion or the facts
we are inconvenienced by
nerve-rending
never-ending
I sense you slipping
into the unconscious state
of sycamore, Silurian
limestone, abstract pus

subfusc the lignite
litany of sulphur
whiff of malefaction, pressurised
organic matter
exhumed to facilitate
all we believe we wish to be
liturgical obfuscation

philosophers often mistake
their failures of imagination
for insight

plummet into the well & welter
of loneliness
she scans
the want ads
subconscious of her wants

declassified advertising like a whole other
life of secret
icons & scepticism

you'd tell me, wouldn't you,
if you really loved me—let's

party to no transgressions
of this freedom
to buy what you are sold

progress is not philosophy—
formal
procedures are needed

we learn by experience
that we meant something
other than we meant to mean

gravestones at Gravelines
a cool brisk breeze blowing
over a relative upland
strip of light, an opening
door way out this way
the catch
in his voice at the point
of departure or
no return: a single point
made inkily in the paper mind
of practical physicians
a thinning point defined
as a single wayward photon
made to exist entirely
without theistic knowledge
by subtle deviation into grain

the silo & factory, bricky, blocky
your futile argument demolished
demobilised, happy as

Mathilde, her matronly elegance
violated by eruptions
of no consequence—the vowel
A is formed by opening
wide the mouth—
I try to remember
as if I ever knew her, as if
she ever existed off
the page of this contemplation

a figure maybe bending in a field
or a balloon, part
deflated caught in the stalks
with a whole life story
some comedy some tragedy of its own
& a future indeterminate
by one listening
who has already passed on

cogent symbols on an incoherent map
the flecks of soil or birdshit now revealed
as markers redolent of city streets
the venues where a population strives
to meet its ends

a blade so cunningly balanced
it recoils as each photon strikes
a slow whirl to power
the fear of birds
a stomach-voiding drop
coeval network of intelligent force
a field full of prominent
mathematicians
grimacing to grasp

the unpremeditated slur
that castigates soft-focus thought
of mere collateral—all this cash
in a virtual vortex
of inane depression

a solitary cormorant flies
an arrow over the site
of the rising stadium
as if this

there is a blunt munificence wherein
this dumb blade
enacts ritual killings
among stocks
& shares the proceeds among

among the mesh
of consequence we tread
on shells, miscalculated
musculature
of valves bleeding the system
under pressure of forgiving forced
to imagine intensity of
entropy in black holes

an unconsidered lifeform
on an undiscovered planet
dying in the instant of its birth

pangs of formation

essences of mud

was you ever bit by a dead bee?

inasmuch as
the foil wrapper
jettisoned in space
flashes its reflections
of another sun
signalling
to a possible people
not yet evolved

fantastic integer of our neurosis
neural credentials
implicit paths

contaminant of imperilled time
this cod aesthetic
plunders valid thought

inside the energy barrier
escaping towards the glass

an error occurred
while processing this directive

*I don't think God
likes free verse*

mesmerise to minimise

a beat or two before we leave the stage

tick

tock

Lamentation

For the destroyer shall come suddenly upon us

that which is manifest begins
with the seed of itself

blurred stirrings
of whatever is new, may be invented

hard black buds of ash,
embers of haw

osier incipient

we weep
on bairns' bones
desolate
            in our own decay

a desert harvest

toxic growth

a language
strangled

Upon the Death of John Barleycorn

for Ric

work with
the grain

nourishment
for children's gaming

church adrift
on fen mist

warmed by candles'
dying fall

oaken buds
excise old leaves

carve the loaf
taste the new word

.

Damaged Mirror

A nocturne in three distressed sonnets

it is the eye where as for this glaucous thing you did not look
at me so & look; because the bone & ash of the root
which raises the unremembered grass
like a piece of the human in the field
the people who do not desire have remembered perhaps
whether almost being, having been ashamed perhaps
the red light of pain reverses the stomach
which shines with pain of the window
exceeds the glitter of all promises in order to deceive the eye
—as for all this, all meanings of being here,
this is not what we mean, they are not here—
an observer of the fear can be deduced perhaps
but shiftless possibility of the mask decreases
the residual importance of the face

as for the blood of dream as seen in the dream mirror
the dream is cold; as for us in necessary marginal
profit of our one self is thought in doubt
concerning the world where it exceeds the story
which is knit because we hide to prove frame
of the reflection where the surface past night
chill of stare at the window is thin; as for us it was
there or anywhere at all; no blood, no blood
at the present surface which is painted
in the wall of night yet you hear the muscle
of your heart in moments of ritual rigorously compressed
the hallucination of image & the impression
continual truth at the time of ceremony
the words more important than the dream

whether I like it or not it is bound to happen
having the rumble threat daily increases
the snow remains lightly but the road is accurate
though curtailment of courses via the bents
is scattered with ash the sky I remember was softer blue
& the waterdrop in the olive drab leaf shines
now brassbound the curtains hang in heavy aspects
reading of old women & the smell of rivers will penetrate
city as the roar of tyres downward of street
that only live in memory the finalisation of cinemas
were a bitter blow I miss the glad upward-illuminated nights
& it forbids now to leave the house until further
at hazard to receive scattered edict
transacted by wireless pronouncings & bound of the tongue

The Penitents

*Seal up those things which the seven thunders uttered
and write them not*

I: Time no longer

processions & parades,
displays of public fervour

the many-coloured madam
manifests divinity

orphreys & precious stones
dalmatic & chasuble over his alb

the fierce & gentle qualities
of suffering

distillation of sanguinity
the corpuscles & the salt

the glimmering world is the past
it flickers in & out of our lives

in a half-crazed round
of nursery songs

penitentiary doors
inlaid with graffiti

gilded columns, ornate
painted & pargetted rooms

the past is everywhere
at either side of the altar

gothic arcading in Manhattan
frescoes rich & modern to the age

processions parade
the darker side of fervour

many-coloured madmen
penitents & flagellants

a man disguised as an animal
peeps at a prostitute with scalloped sleeves

the distinctive sound of psalters
slipped back onto shelves

into the grey uncultivated sky we climb
step by tedious step

edges worn perilous
by pilgrims & the perfect

wicked men attack
divine authority

essences of sanctity & sin—
shameless science exults

II: Lest ye be judged

in taxi-bright city night a priest
wipes hamburger relish on his cassock
a sensual flirtation
with colour
& supersaturated fat
behind shiny glass
jewels borrowed from the Egyptians
chasubles in lightweight Lurex

every world is immutable
the torn & broken edges blurred
thumbed-over ends of bread half-stale
to be cooked again or puddingstone
warmed over

we travel by wagons-lits & tram
not crawling as penitents
but this *is* St Anthony's thumb
or the prepuce of a post-lapsarian divine
—the deep belief of those
who still wear down the stepstones
with their flesh & bones require it

forensics pick for flesh beneath the nail
scratched surfaces of paint
—rood deliverance
from iconic burdens, dyed in the wood—
hold up a glass & see the stains

the castle we enter retains
many aspects of the prison
graffiti in the stonework

god as precursor of CCTV

in his house he will chant impiety
he stripped off his robes
& also prophesied

beware of the scribes

if this is all true I have been betrayed

In Passing

weird August, end of the dry monsoon
in a pot-bellied tramp steamer we speculate on Kandinsky
the cultural attaché & I, deliberate in mufti

culture is always a convenient prostitute
goddess of darkness, mutability & death
unsunned, corpse-white body alluring, not for sale

conical green mountains rise from a coastal plain
full of shadowplay, grotesqueries & lurid colour
smell of foetid bodies in Capricorn heat

Durga with a torn bodice, appellant
delicate flakes of dandruff on a clerical pate
colonial as pipesmoke

**

darkness of the ward at night
the urgent declivity of dreams
amber & jade

a cathedral stillness
tropical torpor
stone haloes & conical hats

fragrant scrub reclaiming the site of a wayside shrine
a cricket chafing song by a patch of oil on gravel
the rhythmic ching of the coppersmith bird

Durga, Uma, Kali; Time & Sleep—
don't jump to any conclusions about this
a candle in an airless empty room

**

her firm white body by him on the bed
remembered shock of the first touch
that alabaster flesh

lights of the valley strung from here to there
a liner lit up on the evening tide
suspicion of music, laughter on the breeze

the boy is abstract
in reflection in the lake
broken up with houses, trees, sky & a votive god

in this political climate
we make our bed & lie—
a difficult berth

**

passion awakes passion
the urgency of sleep in liquid heat
distant noise of engines

rapid eye movements take in the covered market
snow in surprising places
the earnest colloquy of bright brass & leather

wayang voices chatter things you'll never understand
things that should be recalled from dreams
shadows thrown by a kerosene lamp on a screen

to widows leaning on balconies
the endgame is unendurable closure
with a sweep of the hand the dying man

**

in junks & sampans on an inland sea
in strident tones on unseen televisions
idols on the verge of death lay down law

where passing showers of envy snick the skin
puppets of gods are traded at a snack-stop
to leap electrically into possibility

waking with monsters, adult in a child's room
muscular formations of weather beyond the window
reverberate with Thou Shalt Not

the travelling salesman sweeps the cellar steps
blood in newsprint, observation & invention mingled
lub-dub, lub-dub, lub-dub, lub-dub, lub-dub

How Doth the City Sit Solitary

How goodly are thy tents, O Jacob,
thy dwelling places, O Israel

I

How did the place first
become holy? Home to
Shalem, shrine of Baal,
a threshing-floor on the mountain.
The sound of the stone,
the blood of usurpers,
odes to lost children.
Physical splendour alternating
carnage & exultation.

A stretch of that road is visible,
huge blocks of stone. During Passover,
Succoth & Shavuoth,
ox teams hauling
huge slabs of limestone
the sluices of blood, the stench.
In the sanctuary
of churches, mosques & synagogues,
sacred rites of faith
never beyond surveillance.

Signs of messianic redemption,
bleats & bellows of sacrificial animals,
tricky pirouettes. The outline
of the mountain
gradually disappeared.

A lamb for Passover, a bull
for Yom Kippur. This
would have been his path.
Pilgrims spend the night
on the outlying hills,

lights shine from the arches
down its western slope.
The view here is stunning,
five or six coloured hens,
a herd of sheep among scarlet anemones.

II

it was not that they
were so interested
in physics & mathematics

rather that Einstein

human eyes looking
from graves & blood
to a strange glimpse
of the sun's eclipse
a picture
of bending light
shtetl visions
of Chagall

past the public gardens & the house
of culture the rain
began to fall more heavily .

Where Is He That Counted the Towers?

for Barry MacSweeney

I met a traveller of the mythy north
who said to be penetrates especially the manner the word
was built into towers of the hearts of stone
people can predominate landscape or the earth
till the little ones you damn of time you carry all
in order to ruin & newly within the earth
from which all sprang; we drink two & our meaning
how with password, probably rewrite, rightly
to reason were encoded in the very limits of languages
to explain the ways in our spirits & invoke
the histories of a different age must beg
our magic; the story of quern, load-bearing,
to fall with quoin of the church which is forgotten
mulched under again inexorable churn

in effort of totem & summary name of god
or capital people raise their upward stones;
we lift our voices, sing our songs, we say
our tales to justify our to be, return to myths
to instil the primacy of race
beyond the race, legislator beyond the serf, to quell
resistance & abomination, painting
our histories in the weave of the wall;
rocks of the land, vigilance above the sea
of whence we came to where we came to rest;
the return cultic & the Celtic cross
divided by the surf that breaks in main,
the slime, the mud, the reeds, the common tern,
the peep of oystercatchers on the river

And Brake Them Beneath the Mount

the wine-cellar step, the sweat breathed in & out
of smudged & humid walls; pale & small pus butcher's flesh
drips from the collar, rigid the lightened winch
by sausage fingers in the cleft—
the full-filled uniform protracts as the quilted door
of a soundless cell, the microphones embedded,
determined in your stone, temper the pavings,
threaten transfer into tottering position

a big-eyed scholar makes a photogenic
corpse, doll's face in the wreck, a broken board
with the word why half rubbed away: old fuels spent,
old promises; the child, they living, now would be gone
as the fathers whose toil raised a toxic slope,
physics spoiling the child

And the Revolters Are Profound in Slaughter

"Policy without morality cannot be considered serious policy"
—Mikhail Gorbachev

friends bring me orchids
my design is an orchid cemetery

an unmarked grave which citizens
are forbidden to visit

a few inspirational stanzas
then the treadmill

the caucus seethes, a guttering flame
free speech is anathema

the ghosts of failed risings, the only invasion
the farms that fed them, dead ends

the factories that clothed them
copies of the book burned

rusting machinery, flourishing
weeds & snow, toxic gases

emphysema & oxygen bottles
the faithful drawn in millions

by charm & humanity
Occam's razor ruthlessly applied

to a coffin burst open by mourners
a permeable border among buses & trams

intense symbolism
in a wilderness of grass

after the assassination miracles
occurred, not anticipated or planned

shooting is widespread now
as dawn breaks, dying around them

a lone figure carrying a plastic bag
it is thought the secret police

tore pieces from the shroud,
the corpse rolling in the dust

above the altar the declaration:
I am both Abel & Cain

What Then Must We Do

Carthage from the air
the smoking ruins
walls robbed out
trowel scrapes on tesserae
vertiginous descent
through desert sands

Prussian moderne
the broad steps leading down
empty as ransacked tombs
Carthage, then Steglitz

won't look like Chicago
now: jokes with an edge
& the smell of spilled beer
the map redrawn by debris
cataloguing the missing
the early days, before the guilt

a city full of rumours
we protest, they protest
not a game but a measured pavane
an invite to canapés, fingerfood

a homunculus with ghastly teeth
peeks through doors
on inelegance, decadence, laughter of whores

Germany, 1938:
tanks roll
in newsreel glory
making ready

for the end of history
nothing to come
hereafter

a drone that could be overhead
percussive firefight in what passed
for a street, reduced to cabaret scenery

the underground rocket factory
vast fingers poked into the earth
telling stories out of school
nacht und nebel

fingers in that pie
who'll have
the biggest slice
which segment is coloured
red on the chart—& who
gets red in the division
of the legend?

poets & old pros
stagger under this mulch
from the multinational propa-
gator: which side
do we give credit?

a black
market, grubby
tunnellings below
all this weight
of what was domestic
architecture, severed
fingers point
accusing at the sky

Four Distressed Sonnets

I

dull gray & the gray & whose gray of the sky & the land
is sluggish; that with smudged foam & with the birds
of that shouts keening assault of salty air;
where oxidation & wrack decorates the disintegration of husks
of abandoned structures constructed the end to stop
bending the disastrous displacement of the sand,
cuttlebone flotsam, eggs of the seawolf, kelp of the feet,
torn moved away from bags & the plastic other dreck mark
where the swell of the morning the highest lost force
as muscularly the wave disgorges the heaving coast
that receding makes the sea disclose one chainbound corpse
& naked, sexless, discoloured in the inner thigh;
alongside the mud as for outflow of the estuary & which eddies
the subcutaneous bill & you inspect godwits strictly

II

residue mud-brown as convoluted cream;
smell; to harvest it prompts your fingers inside
& consider its treacly, unremovable corruption;
before commemoration, ancient times, time & excess,
half noisome gloop of thing of the shadow,
ephemeral things, gone things before you will
establish or determine them; the melody
perhaps hint which can only be in the ear
of your reason, shading in the past without
possibly always existing in any present;
thistledown you may not grasp; it affects
the intangible walls & unnameable,
continuous that they are not there;
echo of the sound you cannot do

III

the cow drinks crosses the place
in the heavy earth breaks out completely
& still in sky their breath impression
only under the shafts rain now which falls
a hard explicit sky the so much naked soil
sounds as wrapping a dog in closed at
edge of waterhole brilliant with clear
reflected shimmer luminous portrayed dusk
cloud curls vivid pink traces of plane steam
surrounds the domain of wedgewood blue
knee-high mist that wraps the sectors
lighted to the outline of the hill
where see five deer in the daybreak
rigid, alert, regarding, silent, still

IV

the fact that bordered flavour withers of bitterness
the uncultivated land grinds the taste
falling & cuts ploughland to drop, knotty,
the work which fumigates dawns the autumn tongue;
the vulture chaotic spatial flies again
air from the air which gets tangled the bank to fall
spits phlegm warmly fragrant, the border dry fish
good organic savour; each seed of the grass increased
by a droplet; cases of moonlight on the church tower
which goes down, being cut off, dressed silver to the cloud,
that scream of an owl, its constant sparkling wingbeats;
the air coughs & the direction which the wall
cuts the cloud silver stable wingbeats to call;
only the lower part of the tree has the rain

Relics

And they buried him with his fathers in the field

What's all this rancour about?
Life is too precious to keep long.
It is quite dark now & I stumble
at frequent intervals over the dead.

It is strange to be back in the city.
I am not sure the paving can be trusted.
In the church the flowers smell of polish & the candles
of foreign nights after rain.

I feel a peculiar appetite
for buying clothes. The streets are full of people
hawking personal possessions, their own
& other people's bodies,

umbrella handles intricately carved from bones of saints,
fine relics filched from the catacombs.
Who bakes the stars dispatches idiots
to the limits of creed & credence,

our credentials merely all those things
that cannot be disbelieved. What next?
We sing our signs, subsist
for our own recreation

in narratives carefully controlled, constructed
to keep the gullible in thrall.
Call of the ram's horn simulates bare fells,
wind & distance among these clustered streets.

Torch Song

for Penny

blind to the darkness
we brandish our songs
apassionata
in a slow defile

Adalgisa to my Pollione
your flank sleek
under my touch
nape bent beneath curls

to risk redemption
is a sin too far
sinless in the dark
against our mortal selves

a duet of love
sung without words
manuscript
cast to the flames

In Tombland

reticulated tracery, quarried
panes, innocent
of colour
       flushwork
grimy with particulates

poor soul
       at large
in dark alley
ways of intellectual
dead
    ends

tired & foxed, shall we
say £20?
      look up
for a patch of blue
& a primitive
          grotesque
on the cinema tower

no human
      experience
without thought?
no learning
without
     language?
to give a life
of anxiety
     & courage
for such a mis-
conception

touch the decaying
stone
      work
smell the pages

a rigorous, restless
intelligence, end-
                stopt

www.ingramcontent.com/pod-product-compliance
Lightning Source LLC
Chambersburg PA
CBHW031931080426
42734CB00007B/632